# A Powwow Story

Written by Mary Bertucci
Illustrated by Chloe Bluebird Mustooch
Cultural Advice from Bernice Jensen

A Powwow Story
Copyright © 2022 by Mary Bertucci
Illustrated by Chloe Bluebird Mustooch
Cultural Advice from Bernice Jensen

All rights reserved. No part of this publication may be reproduced, distributed, or transmitted in any form or by any means, including photocopying, recording, or other electronic or mechanical methods, without the prior written permission of the author, except in the case of brief quotations embodied in critical reviews and certain other non-commercial uses permitted by copyright law.

Tellwell Talent
www.tellwell.ca

ISBN
978-0-2288-8693-8 (Paperback)
978-0-2288-8694-5 (eBook)

# Table of Contents

Land Acknowledgement ............................................................. v
Hello, Learners! ......................................................................... vii
Collaboration and Many Thanks ............................................. ix
Founder of the Kamloopa Powwow:
    Mary Delores Jules ............................................................. xiii

Chapter 1   A Mountain Morning Drive ..................................1
Chapter 2   Aunt Ruthie ............................................................3
Chapter 3   The Powwow ..........................................................6
Chapter 4   Looking Around ...................................................10
Chapter 5   Teen Girls' Jingle Dance ..................................... 15
Chapter 6   Remembering the Past ....................................... 20
Chapter 7   A Surprise on Sunday .........................................24
Chapter 8   Women's Golden Age Dance ...........................27
Chapter 9   Learning More about Traditions ..................... 32
Chapter 10  Going Home .......................................................34

Useful Vocabulary ....................................................................37
Chapter Questions ...................................................................43
Answer Key ...............................................................................47
Online Resources Consulted ..................................................51

# Land Acknowledgement

With sincere gratitude, I acknowledge that I live, work and wrote this story on the ancestral and unceded territory of the xʷməθkʷəy̓əm (Musqueam), Sḵwx̱wú7mesh (Squamish), səl̓ílwətaʔɬ (Tsleil-Waututh), kʷikʷəƛ̓əm (Kwikwetlem), Stó:lō (Stolo) qiqéyt (Qayqayt), q̓ic̓əy̓ (Katzie) and q'ʷa:n̓ƛ'ən̓ (Kwantlen) Nations. I am deeply grateful to call this place home.

The powwow in this story — Kamloopa — takes place on the ancestral and unceded territory of the Secwépemc people.

Kukwstsétsemc to the Kamloopa Powwow Society and Tk̓emlúps te Secwépemc for allowing this story to be shared.

# Hello, Learners!

My name is Mary Bertucci, and I am a writer and an English language teacher. Nice to meet you! I am very happy to share this story with you. I hope you enjoy reading it. It is a story about family, relationships, community and traditions.

To help you study, there are some extra sections in this book:

1. Useful Vocabulary
2. Chapter Questions
3. Answer Key

Try to read this book without a dictionary. If you don't understand a word, first, look at the vocabulary in the back of the book. Also, use the pictures to help you understand the story. Chloe Bluebird Mustooch is the artist who drew the pictures. She is Indigenous. She comes from the Alexis Nakota Sioux Nation. She knows a lot about powwows and Indigenous traditions! Her drawings will help you understand new words and ideas.

Try the questions at the end of each chapter. You can check your answers using the answer key in the book.

For more activities, practice and information about this story, please visit my website: **marybertucci.ca**.

Good luck with your studies! I hope you like reading about Ben, his family and the powwow.

Happy reading!

# Collaboration and Many Thanks

To all the people who made this story come to life, thank you with all my heart.

| | |
|---|---|
| Story & Activities | **Mary Bertucci**<br>(Ukrainian, Polish, German, Dutch+) |
| Illustrations, Cover & Cultural Perspectives | **Chloe Bluebird Mustooch**<br>(Alexis Nakota Sioux) |
| Cultural Advisor, Traditional Knowledge Sharer & Powwow Dancer | **Bernice Jensen**<br>(Okanagan, Secwépemc) |
| Tk̓emlúps te Secwépemc Elder & Traditional Knowledge Keeper, Administrator of Secwépemc Museum and Heritage Park | **Diena Jules**<br>(Tk̓emlúps te Secwépemc) |
| Tk̓emlúps te Secwépemc Language & Culture Department Advising | **Ted Gottfriedson**<br>**Jessica Arnouse** |

| | |
|---|---|
| Consultation & Story Permissions | **The Kamloopa Powwow Society Delyla Daniels (President)** |
| | **Tk̓emlúps te Secwépemc Chief and Council** |
| | **Alicia John** Executive Secretary to Tk̓emlúps te Secwépemc Chief and Council |
| | **Chief Aileen Prince** (Nak'azdli Whut'en) |
| | **Chief Fred Robbins** (Esk'etemc) |
| Photography Credits | |
| Back Cover - Bernice Jensen | **Derek Rodgers (Gitxsan Photographer)** |
| Back Cover - Mary Bertucci | **Andrea Treviño (Port Coquitlam, B.C.)** |

| | |
|---|---|
| Cultural Perspectives, Feedback & Support (Family) | **Jeremy Lacerte Bertucci** (Nak'azdli Whut'en)<br><br>**Tessula Whitford** (Woodland Cree)<br><br>**Simone Lacerte** (Nak'azdli Whut'en)<br><br>**Jackie Lacerte** (Nak'azdli Whut'en)<br><br>**Rosalie MacDonald** (Lake Babine Nation) |
| Instructor Perspectives & Feedback | **Sylvia Symons**<br>**Vicky Chan-McLean**<br>**Magda Dachtera-Wrobel**<br>**Marie Irving**<br>**Olivia Sullivan** |
| Friend Support & Feedback | **Priya Singh Tronsgard**<br>**Asami Scully-Aranoo**<br>**Claire Flint**<br>**Liz Faulkner**<br>**Marilyn Kennedy** |
| Family Support & Feedback | **Yvonne & Conrad Hynek**<br>**Michel Hynek**<br>**Tracy Hicks**<br>**Grace Kully**<br>**Anne Guenther**<br>**Nico & Sam Bertucci** |

# Founder of the Kamloopa Powwow: Mary Delores Jules

Mary Delores Jules is an Elder of Tk̓emlúps te Secwépemc, and she is a founder of the Kamloopa Powwow. She also served as a home school coordinator and a housing department coordinator, and she was President of the Shuswap Brothers & Sisters Society. Mrs. Jules is also a recipient of the Silver Jubilee Award.

Throughout her life, Mrs. Jules has served her community and worked for the betterment of all First Nations. Her commitment to her community is reflected in her tireless efforts to help bring about change. This is particularly evident in the support she has provided to two of Canada's most well-known and respected Aboriginal leaders: her husband Chief Clarence Jules and her son Chief C.T. (Manny) Jules. She is an inspiration to all who know her, exemplifying unconditional love, support, hard work, pride and community values.

**For Jeremy, Nico & Sam**

Always be proud of who you are.

*MB*

CHAPTER 1
# A Mountain Morning Drive

"Mom, can you tell Danny to turn off his phone? That game is so loud!"

"Danny, turn off the sound, please. It's noisy, and your dad is sleeping."

"Fine." Danny turns off the sound. He looks at Ben and sticks out his tongue. He keeps playing his game.

# A MOUNTAIN MORNING DRIVE

Ben looks out of the car window. It is Saturday morning, and it is very early. The sky is pink and orange. Ben looks at the mountains. They are high and beautiful. Some of them have snow on the top. Others are covered with trees. The trees are tall, old and strong.

Ben is with his family. They live in Port Moody, a city near Vancouver. Today, they are going to a city called Kamloops. His mother, Liv, is driving the car on the highway. She is quietly singing a song. Her eyes are pretty and green. His father, Chris, is sleeping in the front seat. He is a tall man with tattoos on his arms. He is tired because he worked late last night. Ben is sitting beside his younger brother, Danny. Danny is a teenager, and his phone is very important to him.

Ben loves the drive. He is sixteen years old, and he is on summer vacation. He is wearing a baseball jersey. It has his special number on the back – 14. He also has a baseball cap from his team, the Ravens. Ben loves baseball.

The sun starts to rise. It is bright and golden. It is a beautiful day in the Cascade Mountains. It is early, but Ben can't sleep. He is too excited. Today, he is going to his first powwow.

## CHAPTER 2
# Aunt Ruthie

Danny looks up from his phone. "Where are we?" he asks. The car stops outside of a small café.

"We are in Princeton, Danny," his mother says. "Aunt Ruthie is coming with us." Aunt Ruthie is Chris's aunty. She is seventy-four years old. She has long silver hair, and she likes colourful earrings. She lives in Princeton, British Columbia.

Aunt Ruthie is Indigenous. Her mother was Nak'azdli Whut'en. Her father was Esk'etemc. Her people have lived on the land for thousands of years.

Ben loves Aunt Ruthie. She has funny jokes. She knows many things about plants in the forest. Her favourite food is salmon.

# AUNT RUTHIE

Ben looks into the café. Aunt Ruthie is sitting by the window. She sees the car and waves. She has a big smile today. She is wearing her big, colourful earrings with shiny beads. These are her powwow earrings. She comes outside to the car. "Hello, boys! Hi, Liv! Nice to see you."

"Hi, Aunt Ruthie!" everyone replies.

Ben's father gets out of the car, and he gives his aunt a big hug. "I miss you, Aunty! I'm very happy we are going to the powwow together."

"Oh, me too, Chris. I miss you very much. You look good. Liv cooks good food for you boys," Aunt Ruthie says. Chris smiles.

Aunt Ruthie has a big suitcase. Chris puts it in the trunk. Aunt Ruthie sits in the front of the car next to Liv. Ben's dad opens the back door. "Move over, Danny."

"What? Oh, man. The middle seat is so small!" Danny is upset.

"Sorry, son. You're the smallest," Chris replies. Danny moves over. The car is small for three people in the back seat.

Aunt Ruthie turns around. She is smiling. "Ben and Danny, this is your first powwow, isn't it?" asks Aunt Ruthie.

"Yeah," the boys reply.

"I remember my first powwow. It was a long time ago. This is a special time for you boys. You will learn about our culture and traditions."

"Cool," says Danny.

Ben smiles at his younger brother. "Yes, very cool," he says. "I can't wait."

CHAPTER 3
# The Powwow

After about two hours of driving, the family is in Kamloops. It is twelve thirty p.m. Kamloops is a city. It has about 90,000 people. It has many shops, and there is an old part of the city. There is a university there, too. The winters are cold and snowy. The summers are hot and dusty. Today, it is very hot. The temperature is 36°C. Ben is happy he brought his hat and lots of water.

The family drives through the city. Danny has a question. "Aunty, what is a powwow? Is it just dancing?"

"Well, the dances are wonderful, but it is more than dancing. We see our family and friends. We meet dancers and drummers from other places. The songs and dances are prayers and stories. They help us grow strong when we are sick. They help us feel better when we are sad. The powwow is colourful and fun, but it is very important. It keeps our culture alive. It helps us remember who we are."

Ben wants to know more about this culture. He is very interested in his family history and traditions. He doesn't know a lot about his dad's family. They don't live close. Sometimes Ben feels sad about this. He wants more time with his family, so he is always very happy to see Aunt Ruthie.

Soon they come to a bridge. It crosses the South Thompson River. They cross the bridge, and they see many cars, trucks and campers on the other side. "I see it!" Liv says. "Look at all the cars!"

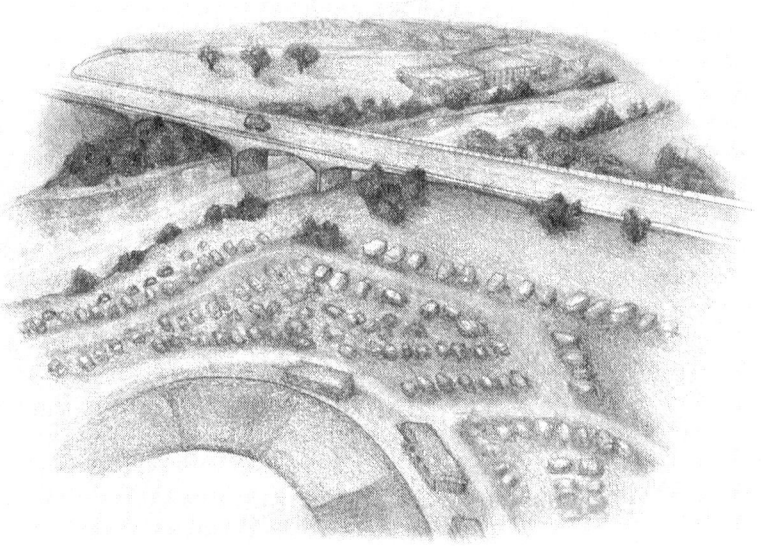

They are on Tk̓emlúps te Secwépemc land. They will be at the powwow soon. It is called the Kamloopa Powwow. Ben feels very excited.

Liv turns right off the highway. She drives a little and turns right again. There is a long line of cars. They wait in the line. "We pay here," says Aunt Ruthie. "It's ten dollars each."

"Okay," says Liv. She takes out her wallet. Soon they are at the front of the line. A volunteer in a red shirt comes to the window.

"Hi there, folks. How many people?"

"Five, please," says Liv. She gives him fifty dollars.

"Thank you," he says. "Enjoy the powwow!"

"Thanks! We will," Liv replies. They drive into a very big parking lot. Liv parks the car. Everyone gets out and stretches their legs. "Remember to wear sunscreen," says Liv.

The sun is very hot. It shines in the blue sky. Ben can feel it on his arms. He puts on sunscreen and gets his water. Danny carries some blankets to sit on.

The family walks together. They see many tents and campers. In the air, Ben smells smoke and food cooking. *People must camp here all weekend*, he thinks. They are close to the powwow now. Then, he hears something. The sound is loud, clear and deep. The beat is like a heart. It is a drum. He hears singing. It is new to him and exciting. He feels something in his chest. It is powerful, and it is strong. Aunt Ruthie looks at Ben. She is smiling. "We are here," she says.

CHAPTER 4
# Looking Around

Ben and the family walk to the entrance. The ground is dusty. The grass is crunchy and dry. Ben steps, and grasshoppers jump high and far. Ben feels very hot. He is sweating. He drinks some water. They get to the entrance, and Ben looks around. "Wow!" he says. He is excited and very curious. He sees many dancers. Their clothes are very colourful. He sees red, blue, green, yellow, orange and purple. Some dancers wear feathers, and others wear furs. They have shawls and beautiful jewelry. He can hear drums and singing.

"Let's walk around," says Chris. "There is so much to see!"

"Sounds good," says Liv. "Let's meet at the burger stand at two p.m. Stay together, boys."

# A POWWOW STORY

Ben and Danny walk around together. There are many tables with art and jewelry. There are women making earrings with colourful beads. There are also tables with clothing and leather shoes called moccasins. Danny sees some t-shirts. The t-shirts have animal art on them. "I like this one with the frog," Danny says to Ben. "I want to get it." He pays twenty-five dollars for the shirt. It is white, and the frog picture is green.

Ben sees some bracelets on a table. They are black and made of leather. He buys one for twenty dollars and puts it on. He will remember his first powwow when he looks at it.

"Are you hungry, Danny?" Ben asks.

"Yeah, super hungry."

"Let's get something to eat. How about some bannock?"

"Yes!" Danny replies. "I love fry bread!" They go to a stand and wait in the long line. "Wow! Everyone wants bannock today," he says. The line moves very slowly.

After some time, they see Aunt Ruthie. She is standing next to a young girl. She looks about six years old. Aunt Ruthie and the girl walk toward Ben and Danny. "Oh, hi, Aunt Ruthie," says Danny.

"Boys," she says, "I want you to meet someone. This is your little cousin. Her name is Tillie."

"Hi," the boys say. Ben and Danny don't know Tillie. She has dark brown hair and brown eyes. She is wearing the clothing of a dancer.

"Are you a dancer?" Ben asks.

"Yeah!" Tillie replies. "It's my first time dancing here." She smiles, and she is missing one front tooth. She looks very cute.

A POWWOW STORY

"Wow! I didn't know that some dancers are so young," says Ben.

"Some of them are old, too!" says Aunt Ruthie. "Anyone can dance!"

Ben smiles. *Even me?* Ben doesn't dance very much.

"Well, let's find your parents, boys. I want to watch the dances now."

"Okay. We will meet you soon. We want to get some bannock," says Ben.

"Oh, good. Get some for your aunty, too. Come on, Tillie." Aunt Ruthie and Tillie walk away together.

"Bye!" says Tillie. She skips away with Aunt Ruthie.

The boys get their fry bread. They walk back to the burger stand. Their parents are waiting for them. Aunt Ruthie is there, too.

"Alright! Let's see some dancing," Chris says. They walk into the arbour together.

CHAPTER 5
# Teen Girls' Jingle Dance

The family is in the arbour. It is very large. It is the shape of a circle. The dancers are in the middle of the circle on the grass. There are drum groups on the outside of the circle. People watch from seats around the circle. It is very crowded. "Look for a place to sit," says Chris. They walk around together.

There are many groups of drummers. One group is beating a large drum. There are ten men drumming and singing together. There is also a young boy with them. He is drumming, too. They play and sing for the dancers. "Wow," says Chris. "They are really good."

Ben loves the sound of the drum. It is very loud. He feels it in his chest.

"Are there any women drummers?" Liv asks Aunt Ruthie.

"Yes, dear. There are some women, but there are more men."

"Oh. Why is that?" asks Liv.

"As I know, it is traditional for men to drum at the powwow," Aunt Ruthie replies. She moves closer to Liv and holds her arm. "But," she says quietly, "I know a drum group with women. They are wonderful and strong," she whispers. Liv and Aunt Ruthie share a little smile.

Finally, Danny sees some seats. They hurry to sit down. "Put the blankets here, Danny. That is how we save our seat," says Aunt Ruthie. Danny puts the blanket down. Now they can watch and relax. A dance is starting. It is a jingle dance.

There are many girls in the circle. They have shiny metal cones on their clothing. They have eagle feathers in their hair. A drum group starts to play and sing, and the girls start to dance. Their feet tap the grass and move quickly to the drum. They bounce, and the small metal cones sound like rain. The metal cones shine in the sunlight. "What a beautiful dance," says Liv.

"And beautiful girls, hey Ben?" says Aunt Ruthie. She smiles and winks at Ben.

"Yes, Aunty. They are very pretty," he says.

Danny looks at his brother. "Ben, your cheeks are red." Danny starts to laugh. Ben feels shy, but the girls are pretty.

Aunt Ruthie tells the family about the dance. "Every dance has a special meaning. When people are sick, a jingle dance makes them feel better. It is a healing dance." Ben thinks about this. He didn't know that dancing is like medicine.

When the dancers finish, everyone claps for them. The family watches different dances for two more hours. They enjoy their time together.

Chris looks at Aunt Ruthie. She looks tired. "Boys, it's time to go," says Chris. "Aunty needs a rest."

"I'm not an old lady," she says to Chris. "But yes, I need a rest."

The family walks back to the car together. They are hot and sleepy. They get into the car, and Chris turns on the air conditioning. "Now that's better!" says Aunt Ruthie. "I was melting out there!" Everyone laughs, and Chris drives back to Kamloops. They are staying in a hotel for the night.

CHAPTER 6

# Remembering the Past

The family checks in at a hotel, and they rest in their rooms for a while. Ben and Danny are sharing a room. "Hey Danny, what do you think of the powwow dancers?" Ben asks.

Danny is lying on the bed. "They are good, I guess. It's not my kind of dance. Hip-hop is way cooler." Danny likes cool things.

"I really like the drums. I would love to learn drumming one day," says Ben.

"Yeah, sure," says Danny. He is busy on his phone. He is usually on his phone.

The boys hear a knock at the door. It is their mom. "Time for dinner! Do you guys want to go for sushi?"

"Yeah!" they reply.

"I'm so hungry!" says Danny.

"You're always hungry," says Ben.

"Yeah, I am," says Danny with a smile. They put on their shoes and leave the room.

The family drives to a sushi restaurant in Kamloops. It is called Sushi Aranoo. Ben wonders if Aunt Ruthie eats sushi. "Aunty, do you like sushi?" he asks.

"Can I have salmon?"

"Yeah."

"Then I think I like sushi." Aunt Ruthie laughs. It is a big loud laugh. It always makes Ben happy.

The family sits down and orders some food. They try different rolls, miso soup, tempura and noodles.

They talk, eat and enjoy their dinner. They start to eat some dessert – chocolate ice cream. It is Aunt Ruthie's favourite. Then Aunt Ruthie looks at Chris. She asks a question. "So, Chris, my nephew, why don't you come to see me anymore?" Chris stops eating his dessert. He looks a little uncomfortable.

"Well, Aunty, you know. Life is busy in the city. It's hard to find free time." Ben knows that his parents are very busy. They work hard every day. His dad has two jobs. It is expensive to live in Port Moody.

Aunt Ruthie smiles a little. "I know the city is a busy place. It's too busy sometimes." She is quiet for a minute. "Do you remember when you were young, Chris? You stayed with me and your Uncle James in Merritt every summer." Ben doesn't know about this. His dad doesn't talk about his childhood very much. "Boys, your father always helped us with our salmon. One year, we got thirty fish for our family. We cleaned salmon all day and all night. We dried some salmon and smoked some salmon. Do you remember, Chris?"

Chris has a smile on his face. "Yes, Aunty. Of course I do! My hands smelled like fish for a week!"

Aunt Ruthie laughs loudly. "You are a good nephew – maybe my favourite one."

"Maybe?" Now Chris laughs.

"That was a special time. You learned our traditions in the summer. Don't forget them, Chris. You need traditions. We all need them. You have to teach your boys the things you remember."

"I know, Aunty. I know." Chris looks down at his ice cream.

Danny is texting. He stops and looks at his dad. "You really cleaned thirty salmon, Dad?"

Chris looks at Danny. "Yeah, I did," he says. "I can teach you guys if you want to learn."

"Yeah. That would be cool, Dad," says Danny.

Chris looks at his two boys. He smiles. Ben smiles, too. Cleaning fish is a family tradition. *Yeah, I could learn that*, Ben thinks. He wonders what other things he can learn this summer.

CHAPTER 7
# A Surprise on Sunday

Ben wakes up at eight a.m. He feels good after a long sleep. He and Danny shower and get dressed. They go downstairs to the small hotel dining room for breakfast. It is warm and busy. It smells like coffee and bacon. There are many people eating breakfast at the tables. They are eating bacon, eggs, croissants, pancakes and yogurt.

The boys get some breakfast. They see their family at a table. Aunt Ruthie is drinking tea, and Ben's parents are drinking coffee. They are talking, but they stop when the boys come over. "Shhhh," says Aunt Ruthie. She looks at Ben and Danny. "Good morning," she says.

"Morning, Aunty," they reply. They sit down and start to eat breakfast. Ben is very hungry.

"I have a surprise for you boys," says Aunt Ruthie. "We are going back to the powwow today. I want you to see a few more dances."

"Nice!" says Ben.

"We are leaving at noon, so please be ready to go at eleven forty-five," says Liv. "We can't be late today."

"Why?" asks Ben.

"You'll see," says Aunt Ruthie. She is smiling. Ben wonders what is going on. *Is there another surprise?*

After breakfast, the boys change into their swimming shorts. They go downstairs to the outdoor pool. There are some children playing in the water.

Ben and Danny love to swim. Danny runs and jumps into the pool. He makes a big splash, and the children scream. Danny laughs and starts swimming. Ben loves Danny. He is outgoing and fun. Ben is quiet and a little shy. Sometimes he wants to be like Danny. He steps into the water. It feels cold, but it is nice. The sun is getting hot. It is supposed to be 38°C today. Ben floats in the water, and he feels relaxed.

After about one hour, Ben and Danny see Aunt Ruthie. "Aunty, do you want to swim with us?" Danny asks.

"No thank you, Danny. I don't like the pool smell. The lake is where I like to swim."

"Okay," Danny says.

"You need to shower before we go," says Aunt Ruthie. "Do you know it's eleven thirty?"

"What?!" They boys jump out of the water. They are late!

"Oh, just kidding!" says Aunt Ruthie. "It's only eleven!" She laughs her big laugh again and walks away. Ben looks at her and laughs, too. *She's tricky*, thinks Ben. He loves it.

CHAPTER 8

# Women's Golden Age Dance

The family arrives at the powwow at twelve thirty p.m. The line of cars is long again. They wait and enjoy the cool air conditioning in the car. Chris pays a volunteer fifty dollars, and they enter the parking lot. He parks the car, and the family walks to the entrance. Chris has Aunt Ruthie's suitcase. *Why does Dad have the suitcase?* thinks Ben. *That is strange...*

It is another busy day at the powwow. It is very hot and windy. There are many people walking around – dancers, drummers, families. Ben sees people who do not look Indigenous. *Are they Indigenous?* Maybe they are, but Ben isn't sure. Aunt Ruthie says everyone is welcome at powwows. *Maybe they also want to learn about history and culture*, Ben thinks. *It is nice that everyone can come and learn together.*

Suddenly, Ben hears Danny. "Dad, where is Aunt Ruthie?" he asks.

"Oh, she has something important to do," he says. "She'll be back soon." The family decides to have lunch. They buy some hot dogs and fries and eat together.

## WOMEN'S GOLDEN AGE DANCE

After lunch, they enter the arbour and look for seats. Today, it is not easy. They can't find a place to sit down. Ben is looking around. Suddenly, he sees Aunt Ruthie, but she looks different. She is dressed like a dancer!

"Hey, Dad!" says Ben. "Look at Aunt Ruthie!" He points to her, and Danny is also surprised. The family walks over to see her.

"Do you like my regalia?" Aunt Ruthie asks. She shows the boys her dancer's clothing. It is mostly made of soft leather called buckskin. The leather is the colour of cream. She has a shawl around her shoulders. It is white with some blue and yellow flower designs. There are long thin pieces of buckskin on the edge of her shawl. There are many shiny beads on her shawl as well. They sparkle in the sunlight. Her moccasins have beads, too. These shoes look soft and comfortable. She has big earrings made of many small beads. She wears an eagle feather in her long, braided hair. She holds a fan made of eagle feathers in her right hand.

"I am dancing today, boys. I wanted to surprise you." The boys look very surprised. Just then, someone calls the dancers to the circle. The people watching from the seats stand up. Aunt Ruthie looks at Danny and Ben, smiles and winks.

Aunt Ruthie walks onto the grass. She takes a deep breath. Her back is straight. Her face changes. She looks calm and strong. Now, she is ready to dance.

There are seventeen women in the circle. They are older. Many of them look like aunties and grandmas. Each one has different regalia. They wait for the drum.

A drum starts beating. Singers begin their song. The women begin their dance. Ben watches Aunt Ruthie. She sways softly to the music of the drum. She taps her feet on the grass – *tap*, tap, *tap*, tap, *tap*, tap. She connects to the Earth. The long leather pieces on her shawl move with her – back and forth, back and forth. She raises her fan made of eagle feathers. *She looks like a leader – like a queen – but not a queen*, thinks Ben...

She is an Elder. She is wise, and she is strong. She understands the teachings of her people. She teaches others, and the culture stays alive. Her spirit is beautiful. Ben watches her dance, and his heart feels very full. Ben is proud that Aunt Ruthie is his family. Ben is proud to be Indigenous.

The women dance for a long time. It is very hot, but they keep dancing. Then the music stops. The dance is finished. The crowd claps and cheers for the dancers, and the women leave the grass. The family walks over to Aunt Ruthie. She looks very hot, but she is happy. Ben gives her some water.

"Aunty, that was amazing! You were great!" says Ben. "I didn't know you dance."

"Yes, Ben. It is part of who I am. It is how I keep our traditions in my life. It makes my spirit strong."

Ben smiles. *I need more time with Aunt Ruthie*, he thinks. He has a lot to learn.

"Aunty?" Ben says. "Can I take a picture with you? I want to remember your dance and everything today."

"Yes, Ben, and thank you for asking. It is respectful to ask dancers before you take a picture. Danny, can you take it for us? You are good with your phone."

Danny smiles. "Sure, Aunty!" Ben and Aunt Ruthie stand together. Danny takes a few pictures. Everyone will remember this day.

CHAPTER 9

# Learning More about Traditions

After three more hours at the powwow, the family is ready to go home. Aunt Ruthie changes into her other clothes. They pack her suitcase in the car. They drive back to Princeton. They talk, eat snacks and relax.

"Aunt Ruthie," says Liv. "How did you choose your clothing for the dance?"

"Oh, well it took a long time to collect the pieces," replies Aunt Ruthie. "Uncle James gave me my earrings. The shawl was a gift from my friend. I bought the moccasins to match. It took many years to get everything."

"Yeah, there are so many pieces! It looks hard to make," says Liv. "It must take a long time to make the costumes."

"Yes, it takes a very long time. Actually, we call it regalia, dear, not costumes. Costumes are for Halloween."

"Oh! I'm so sorry, Aunty. I didn't know that..." Liv looks worried.

"It's okay, Liv." Aunt Ruthie smiles. "You are learning." She looks out the window. "Many people are learning about us now — about the beautiful things and the terrible, sad things we have lived through. There are many stories to tell. The stories are important. It is good to listen. I like that you ask me questions, Liv. I like that you listen to the answers with your heart."

Liv smiles at Aunt Ruthie. A tear is on her cheek. She holds Aunt Ruthie's hand.

Ben has so many questions. He is curious like his mother, but sometimes it is hard to ask questions. *I will try*, thinks Ben. *If I want to learn, I need to ask and listen.*

CHAPTER 10

# Going Home

At seven p.m., the family arrives in Princeton. They stop in front of Aunt Ruthie's house. Everyone gets out of the car.

Chris walks over to Aunt Ruthie and hugs her first. "Thank you for coming with us, Aunty," says Chris. "Your dance was very special. I forgot some things – important things. Thank you for helping me remember. I hope we can all go to the powwow again next year."

"Me too, Chris. Take care of yourself and your family, and call your aunty sometime."

Chris laughs. "Yes, Aunty," he says.

Liv and Danny give Aunt Ruthie hugs next. Ben waits until they are finished saying goodbye. Finally, it is his turn.

He walks up to Aunt Ruthie and gives her a big hug. It is a long hug. He doesn't want to let her go.

"Did you enjoy the powwow, Ben?" she asks.

"Yeah, Aunty. I loved it." He steps back and looks at Aunt Ruthie. She is smiling. He loves that smile. Ben takes a deep breath and asks his question. "Aunty,

I want to know more about our traditions, about our family and about your life. Can I come back this summer and stay with you for a few days? Like Dad used to?"

"Yes, of course you can, Ben! Wow, that idea makes me so happy! You are always welcome, Ben. You are family." Ben sees tears in her eyes, and they hug again. "We have a lot to talk about," she says. "Yes, this will be good for everyone. Oh, and Ben, bring your little brother with you. He can learn a few things, too." Aunt Ruthie winks, and they both smile.

After one more big hug, Ben gets back in the car. Everyone waves goodbye. Ben watches Aunt Ruthie until she disappears.

The family drives back through the Cascade Mountains. Ben sees these mountains with snow on the top. He sees the trees that are tall, old and strong. The bright sun sets slowly behind the mountains. The sky is pink and orange.

Ben looks out the window again. He remembers the drums, the beat like a heart. He takes another deep breath. Today, Ben understands something. His family comes from this land. These traditions are his, too. Today, Ben knows this land is home.

# Useful Vocabulary

**air conditioning** – a machine or part of a car used to cool down the air on hot days; also called A/C

**arbour** – an outdoor place where many people can come together; it is in the shape of a circle and has a roof with a hole in the middle

**back and forth** – moving from back to front, like a child's swing

**bannock** – a kind of fried bread; it was introduced to Indigenous Peoples by the Scottish in the eighteenth and nineteenth centuries

**beads** – small round pieces of bone, shell, plastic or glass with holes in the middle; used to make jewelry and art

**bracelet** – a type of jewelry worn on the wrist

**braid** – a way to style hair by crossing over pieces of hair many times

**bridge** – a structure that connects two sides together, often over water

**buckskin** – soft, strong leather made of deer or sometimes sheepskin

**calm** – relaxed

**Cascade Mountains** – the mountains between Vancouver and Kamloops; not the same as the Rocky Mountains

**cone** – something in the shape of an ice cream cone

**connect** – to make two things touch; to make things come together

**croissant** – a kind of pastry

**culture** – traditions and the special ways that groups of people live

**designs** – art

**drummers** – people who play drums

**eagle** – a large strong bird that eats small animals and fish; eagles are important in Indigenous cultures

**Elders** –Indigenous people who are very wise and share important information about culture and traditions with younger people

**Esk'etemc** – A First Nation band northwest of Kamloops; they are part of the Secwépemc Nation

**float** – to rest on top of the water; to be in the air without falling down

**fur** – the hair on animals

**gate –** a place where people stop before going inside; they might pay money here to go inside

**Indigenous –** the first people who lived on the land we call North America and their living family members today

**jewelry –** accessories people wear like earrings, rings, necklaces and bracelets

**jingle dance –** a kind of powwow dance; metal cones on the dress make a sound like rain; a healing dance

**joke –** to do or say something that makes people laugh; also a trick

**Kamloopa –** the name of the powwow that happens every August long weekend at Tk̓emlúps te Secwépemc

**Land Acknowledgement –** a sentence to respect and remember that today, people live on the land that Indigenous Peoples have lived on for thousands of years

**moccasins –** special soft boots made of leather; a kind of traditional Indigenous clothing

**Nak'azdli Whut'en –** a First Nation band in the north of British Columbia; they are part of the Carrier Nation of the Déné

**powwow** – a cultural festival with singing, drumming, dancing and eating; powwows are important in Indigenous cultures

**powwow grounds** – the land where the powwow happens

**prayers** – asking for help from a god or powerful spirit; saying thank you to a god or spirit

**regalia** – traditional clothing worn by dancers at powwows; not the same as a costume

**shawl** – a piece of clothing; it goes around the shoulders like a big scarf

**spirit** – the part a person that is not their body; their soul

**tattoos** – art printed on people's bodies with special ink

**tents and campers** – places to sleep in outside; used for camping

**Tk̓emlúps te Secwépemc** – the land where the Tk̓emlúps te Secwépemc people live; the Secwépemc people are Indigenous

**trunk** – the back of a car where suitcases can go

**sunscreen** – a kind of cream or spray people use to protect their skin from the sun

**volunteer** – a person who works for free

**wink** – to close one eye quickly; in body language, it can mean something is a secret or a joke

# Chapter Questions

Use the book to answer these questions. You can write a full sentence of your own or key word answers. Key words are the most important words in a sentence.

### Chapter 1
1. Why does the mom want Danny to turn off the sound?
2. Who is in the car? Where are they going?
3. What sport does Ben like? How do you know?
4. Why can't Ben sleep?

### Chapter 2
1. Who is Aunt Ruthie?
2. Where does Aunt Ruthie live?
3. Why is Danny upset?
4. What will the powwow teach the boys?

### Chapter 3
1. Write three things about Kamloops.
2. When they cross the bridge, what land is the family on?
3. What are two things that people do at powwows?
4. What does Ben smell? What does he hear?

### Chapter 4
1. What do the dancers wear? Name three things.
2. What does Danny buy at the powwow?
3. Who is standing by Aunt Ruthie? Who is she?
4. Who can dance at powwows?

**Chapter 5**
1. How many men are beating the drum?
2. What kind of dance does the family watch?
3. What do the metal cones on the clothing sound like?
4. Why are Ben's cheeks red?

**Chapter 6**
1. Does Danny like the powwow dancers? Why or why not?
2. Where does the family go for dinner? What do they eat?
3. Who did Chris see every summer as a child?
4. What things did Chris learn to do with Aunt Ruthie and Uncle James?

**Chapter 7**
1. What are people eating for breakfast?
2. Where is the family going on Sunday (today)? Why?
3. Describe Danny's personality. Describe Ben's personality.
4. Aunt Ruthie jokes with the boys. What is her joke?

**Chapter 8**
1. What does Ben think is strange?
2. Where are there beads on Aunt Ruthie's clothing? Give three examples.
3. What is the surprise?
4. Why does Aunt Ruthie dance?

**Chapter 9**
1. For how many hours does the family stay at the powwow?
2. Who gave Aunt Ruthie her shawl?
3. What does Liv call the dancers' clothing? Is this the right word?
4. Is Aunt Ruthie angry at Liv? How do you know?

**Chapter 10**
1. Why does Ben want to stay with Aunt Ruthie this summer?
2. Does Aunt Ruthie want Ben to come and stay with her?
3. How does she feel about Ben's idea?
4. What new things does Ben understand?

# Answer Key

These are the answers to the questions. They are in *key words* – the most important words in a sentence. You can make full sentences in your *own* words for more practice. Make sure to have a subject, a verb and an object!

For example:

**Q1. Why does the mom want Danny to turn off the sound?**

Key words: phone – noisy and loud, dad sleeping

Sentences: The phone is noisy and loud. The dad is sleeping.

## Chapter 1
1. phone – noisy and loud, dad sleeping
2. Ben, Danny, Liv Chris; going to Kamloops / to a powwow
3. baseball; wears baseball jersey and baseball hat
4. feels too excited (about the powwow)

## Chapter 2
1. Chris' aunty
2. Princeton
3. has to sit in middle seat, very small seat
4. about their culture, traditions

## Chapter 3
1. has about 90,000 people, many shops, old part of city, has university; winters cold, snowy; summers hot, dusty
2. Tk'emlúps te Secwépemc land
3. dance; see family and friends; meet dancers, drummers from other places; remember who they are; remember stories of their culture
4. smells – smoke, food cooking; hears – a drum, singing

## Chapter 4
1. colourful clothing; feathers, furs, shawls, jewelry
2. white t-shirt with green frog on it
3. Tillie – Ben and Danny's cousin
4. anyone; young and old people

## Chapter 5
1. ten
2. jingle dance
3. rain
4. feels shy to say girls are pretty

## Chapter 6
1. yes – good, but not his kind of dance; likes hip-hop better
2. sushi restaurant called Sushi Aranoo; eat rolls, miso soup, tempura, noodles, chocolate ice cream
3. Aunt Ruthie and Uncle James
4. clean salmon, dry and smoke salmon; other traditions

## Chapter 7
1. bacon, eggs, croissants, pancakes, yogurt (not coffee, tea – these are *drinks*!)
2. back to the powwow; going to see more dances
3. Danny – outgoing, fun; Ben – quiet, a little shy
4. tells them they are late, not really late

## Chapter 8
1. his dad (Chris) has Aunt Ruthie's suitcase at powwow
2. on her clothing, shawl, moccasins, big earrings
3. Aunt Ruthie – dancing in the powwow!
4. part of who she is; how she keeps traditions in her life, makes her spirit strong

## Chapter 9
1. three hours
2. her friend
3. costume; no – called regalia, not costume
4. no – smiles at Liv, likes Liv's questions

## Chapter 10
1. wants to know more about traditions, his family, Aunt Ruthie's life
2. yes
3. feels so happy, will be good for everyone
4. family, Ben comes from the land, land – home

**Notes:**

# Online Resources Consulted

Websites and videos consulted while researching story content:

1. First Nations Territory Map
   http://www.museevirtuel-virtualmuseum.ca/sgc-cms/expositions-exhibitions/bill_reid/english/resources/map.html

2. Living By the Drum - Episode 4: Kamloopa, Kamloops, BC (APTN Canada)
   https://www.youtube.com/watch?v=KB3ITbJ24ZM

3. Kamloopa Powwow on YouTube
   https://www.youtube.com/watch?v=KB3ITbJ24ZM

4. Jingle Dance
   https://www.ammsa.com/publications/windspeaker/healing-gift-jingle-dance
   https://www.youtube.com/watch?v=gk7Cha5BVUc

5. Powwow Dance Regalia (CBC)
   https://www.youtube.com/watch?v=UW4bRebdPws

6. Article on Women Drumming at Powwows
   https://windspeaker.com/node/8873#:~:text=Fight%20back'.%E2%80%9D&text=Can%20traditional%20spiritual%20practice%20change,drumming%20at%20their%20local%20powwow

7. Useful Vocabulary Page
*Bannock*
https://www.youtube.com/watch?v=rM-n0U-7wmA
(Bernice Jensen)

*Esk'etemc*
https://www.esketemc.ca/about-us/

*Elders*
https://www.oise.utoronto.ca/deepeningknowledge/Teacher_Resources/Curriculum_Resources_%28by_subjects%29/Social_Sciences_and_Humanities/Elders.html

*Nak'azdli Whut'en*
https://nakazdli.wpcomstaging.com

*Tk̓emlúps te Secwépemc*
https://tkemlups.ca/profile/history/our-land/

Manufactured by Amazon.ca
Bolton, ON